Parenting for Academic Success
A Curriculum for Families Learning English

Unit 3:
Family Stories

PARENT WORKBOOK

Lesson 1: Making Family Connections

Lesson 2: Sharing Family Stories

National Center for Family Literacy

 DELTA PUBLISHING COMPANY

Copyright © 2005 by the National Center for Family Literacy

All rights reserved. No part of this publication may be reproduced or transmitted in any form or by any means, electronic or mechanical, including photocopying, recording, or any information storage and retrieval system, without permission in writing from the publisher.

Requests for permission to make copies of any part of the work should be sent to:

DELTA PUBLISHING COMPANY
A Divison of DELTA SYSTEMS CO., INC.
6213 Factory Road-Unit B
Crystal Lake, IL 60014 USA
(800) 323-8270 or (815) 363-3582
www.delta-systems.com

Printed in the United States of America

Parent Workbook 3   ISBN-10: 1-932748-31-8
                      ISBN-13: 978-1-932748-31-4

Acknowledgments

Parenting for Academic Success: A Curriculum for Families Learning English was developed by the National Center for Family Literacy (NCFL) in collaboration with the Center for Applied Linguistics (CAL) and K. Lynn Savage, English as a Second Language (ESL) Teacher and Training Consultant.

Principle Curriculum Authors: Janet M. Fulton (NCFL), Laura Golden (CAL), Dr. Betty Ansin Smallwood (CAL), and K. Lynn Savage, Educational Consultant.

Special thanks to the Toyota Family Literacy Program, which piloted these materials in Washington, DC; New York, NY: Providence, RI; Chicago, IL; and Los Angeles, CA.

The Verizon Foundation provided original funding for the development of this curriculum and supports the National Center for Family Literacy in its development of resources for English language learners. Verizon's support of the literacy cause includes Thinkfinity.org, a free digital learning platform that advances learning in traditional settings and beyond the classroom. Visit the Thinkfinity Literacy Network managed by the National Center for Family Literacy and ProLiteracy Worldwide on Thinkfinity.org for free online courses and resources that support literacy across the life span.

Special thanks to Jennifer McMaster (NCFL) for her editing expertise.

A Message for Parents

This program is designed for parents who want to build their English language skills. The program also will help you learn ways to help your child improve his or her skills to succeed in school.

You will do activities to learn and practice reading, writing, speaking and listening in English. These activities also share information about how children learn to speak and read English. Each lesson has an activity you can do with your child at home.

When you support your child's learning at home, your child learns how language works.

Doing family learning activities together:

- Helps you be your child's first teacher.
- Helps you learn how your child learns.
- Makes learning fun.
- Supports your child's learning outside the classroom.

You can help your child learn every day. This program will help you help your child to learn.

Un Mensaje para Padres

Este programa está creado para padres que quieren mejorar sus destrezas en inglés. A la misma vez el programa les va a ayudar apoyar el aprendizaje de sus niños y a prepararlos para tener éxito escolar cuando entran a las escuelas.

Dentro encontrarán actividades para que mejoren sus destrezas de lectura, escritura, y conversación en inglés. Las actividades van a compartir información acerca de cómo aprenden los niños a hablar y leer en inglés. Cada lección tiene actividades para hacer en casa con sus niños.

Cuando usted apoya el aprendizaje de su niño en casa, él o ella aprende como se usa el lenguaje.

Cuando hacen actividades escolares juntos:

- Le ayuda ser el primer maestro de su niño.
- Le ayuda aprender como aprende su niño.
- Aprendiendo conceptos es más divertido.
- Apoya el aprendizaje de su niño fuera del salón de clase.

Le puede ayudar a su niño diariamente. Este programa le ayuda apoyar el aprendizaje de su niño.

LESSON 1

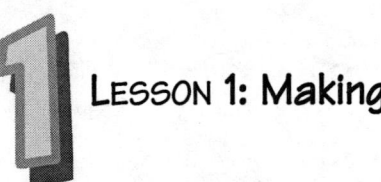

Lesson 1: Making Family Connections

Lesson Goal
Talk about family members and family heritage and share family stories to build language and literacy skills.

Lesson Objectives
Today we will:

- ▶ Talk about family stories.
- ▶ Tell family stories.
- ▶ Practice family vocabulary.
- ▶ Learn one way to help tell family stories.
- ▶ Review and think about what we learned together.

Lesson Warm–Up

1. Listen while your teacher reads this story.

Family Story: Empanadas

Once a year my Aunt Paz and Uncle Beto would make dozens and dozens of *empanadas*, [calabaza] sweet turnovers filled with sweet potato or squash from their garden. They would invite all the relatives and friends to come over, and you could eat as many as you wanted. They lived in a little one–bedroom house, and every surface in the house was covered with plates of *empanadas*. There was no place to sit down.

There's <u>Uncle</u> Beto, rolling out the dough. <u>Aunt</u> Paz, in the yellow dress with red flowers, is spreading the filling. My <u>mother</u> and <u>father</u> are drinking coffee. That's <u>me</u> in the blue dress.

Reprinted with permission of the publisher, Children's Book Press, San Francisco, CA, www.childrensbookpress.org. *In My Family/En mi familia* copyright © 1996 by Carmen Lomas Garza.

UNIT 3: Family Stories

LESSON 1

2. Think, Draw, Pair, Share.
    ▸ Think of a childhood memory. (*Think*)
    ▸ Draw a picture in the box below to show that memory. (*Draw*)
    ▸ Discuss your family story with a partner. (*Pair*)
    ▸ Share your ideas with the class or small group. (*Share*)

3. Answer the questions below.
    ▸ What stories did your family tell when you were a child?

    We told stories about My mom like the cook in the kichen only mom for my I see for my .

    ▸ What stories do you tell in your family now?

    We tell stories about _____
    _____.

2 Parenting for Academic Success

LESSON 1

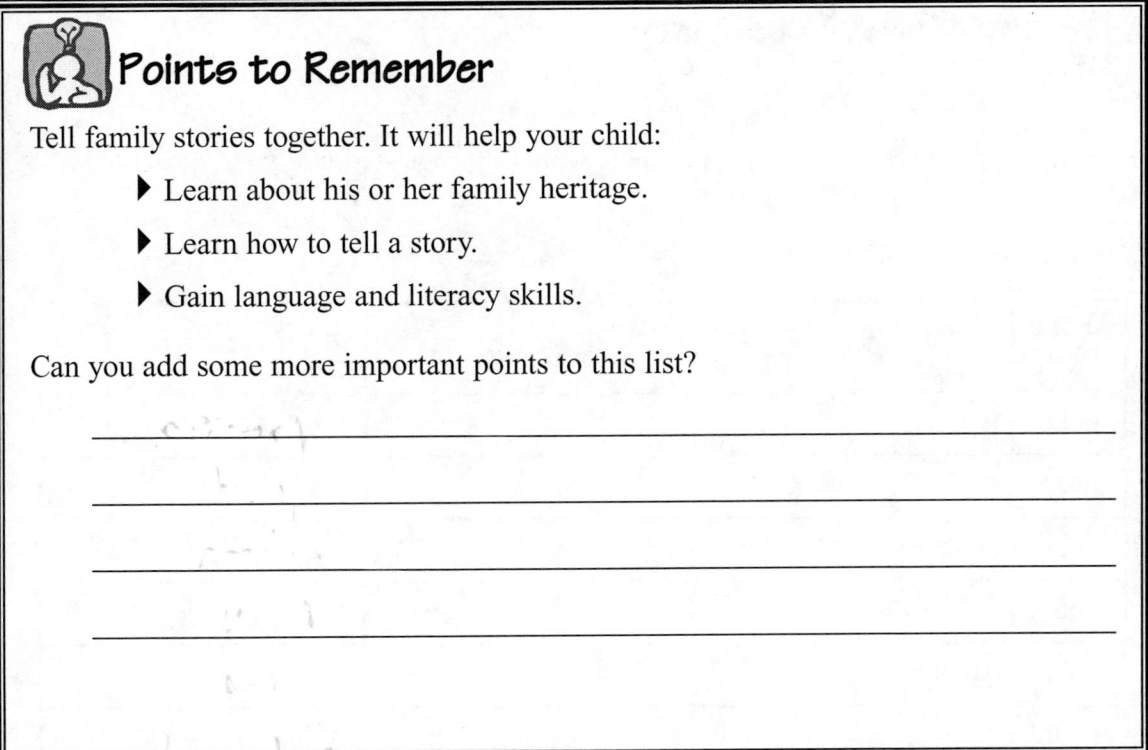

Points to Remember

Tell family stories together. It will help your child:

- Learn about his or her family heritage.
- Learn how to tell a story.
- Gain language and literacy skills.

Can you add some more important points to this list?

_____

_____

_____

_____

UNIT 3: Family Stories

LESSON 1

 ACTIVITY 1: Key Vocabulary

Words in this lesson are listed below. Use the Key Vocabulary pages to build your vocabulary.

1. Review the words. Which ones do you know?

Word Part	Word	Example	Translation
noun	family		familia
noun	father		padre pápa
noun	mother		máma
noun	child		hijos
noun	daughter		niña
noun	sister		hermana
noun	son		hijo
noun	brother		hermano
noun	uncle		tio
noun	aunt		tia
noun	cousin		prima
noun	niece		sobrina
noun	nephew		sobrino
noun	grandmother		abuela
noun	grandfather		buelo
noun	great–grandmother		bisabuelo
noun	great–grandfather		bisabuela
noun	family stories		historia de familia
noun	family tree		familia de trees
noun	family circle		toda la familia

4   Parenting for Academic Success

LESSON 1

2. Practice using Key Vocabulary words. Finish these sentences.

My mother's name is __Yesenia Alfaro__.

My father's name is __William Pacheco__.

My daughter's name is __Marjorie Pacheco__.

My son's name is __William Pacheco__.

My grandmother's name is __Teresa Bolaños__ (my mother's mother).

My grandfather's name is __Alfredo Escobar__ (my mother's father).

My grandmother's name is __Lucia Alfaro__ (my father's mother).

My grandfather's name is __Tonio Escobar__ (my father's father).

My aunts' names are __Doris Escobar__.

My uncles' names are __Fredy Bolaños__.

My cousins' names are __Daniel Escobar__.

Other important family members:

_____ (name) _____ (relationship)

_____ (name) _____ (relationship)

_____ (name) _____ (relationship)

_____ (name) _____ (relationship)

_____ (name) _____ (relationship)

UNIT 3: Family Stories

LESSON 1

Activity 2: Making a Family Picture

Family Circle

1. A family circle is a drawing of a family. Complete your family circle.
   - Write your name in the circle labeled "My Name."
   - Write the names of your children in the circle labeled "My Children."
   - Write the names of your brothers and sisters in the circle labeled "My Brothers and Sisters."
   - Write the name of your parents in the circle labeled "My Parents."
   - Write the names of other family members in the circle labeled "Other Relatives."

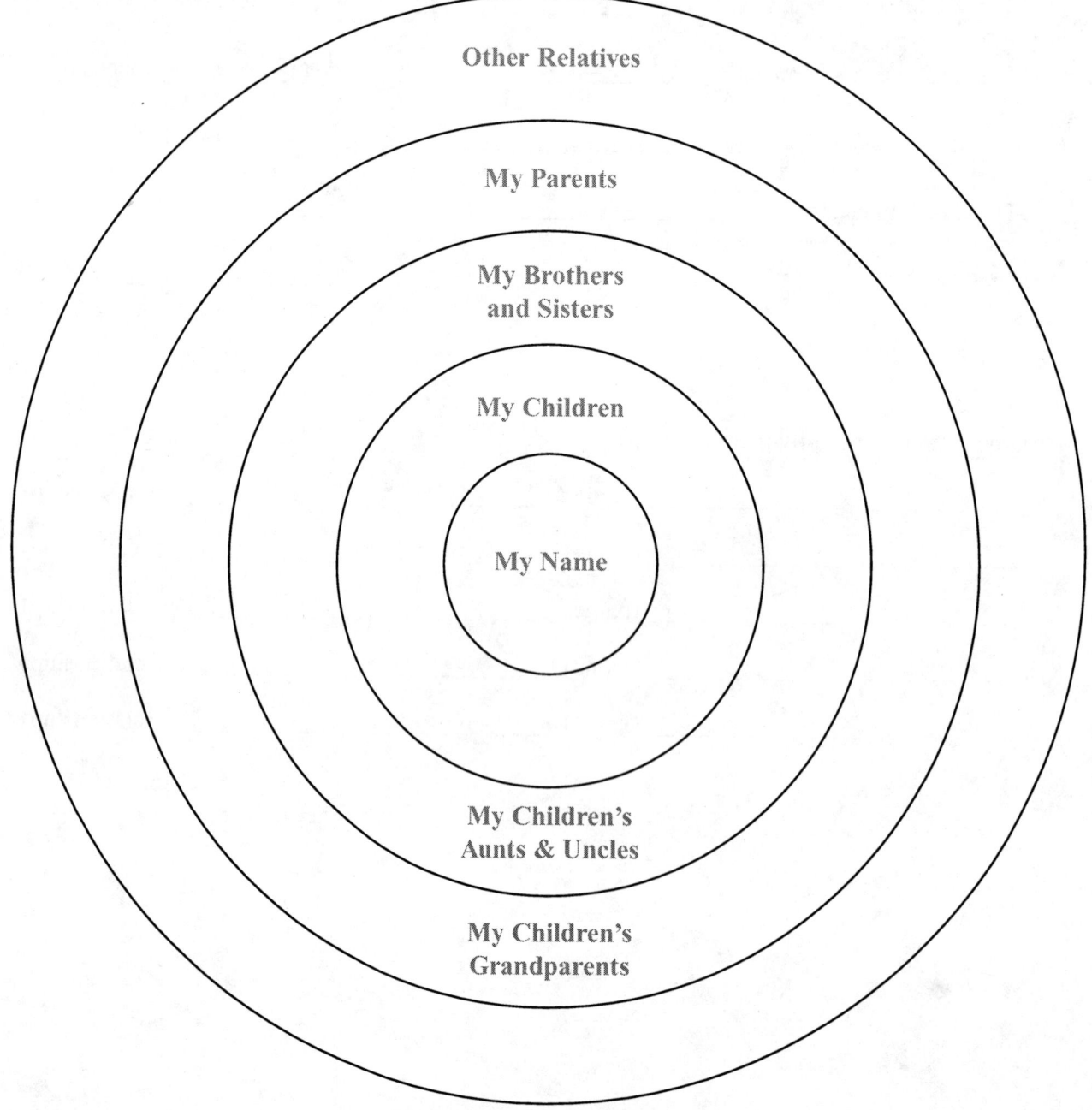

Parenting for Academic Success

LESSON 1

Family Tree

1. A family tree is a drawing of a family. Complete your family tree.
   - Write your name in the box labeled "My Name."
   - Write the names of other family members in the other boxes.

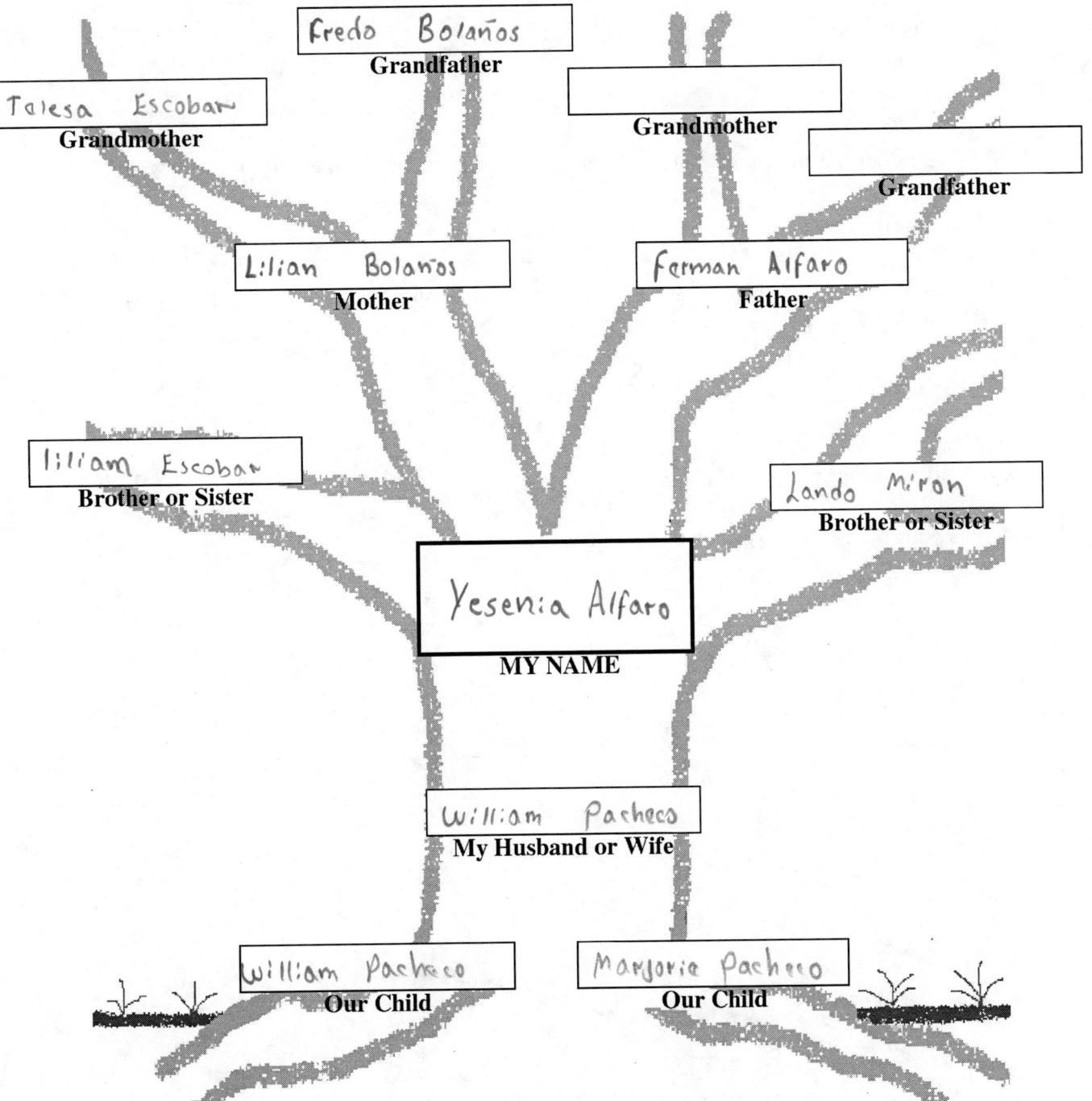

UNIT 3: Family Stories

LESSON 1

ACTIVITY 3: Sharing Your Family Picture

1. Show your family circle or family tree to a partner.

2. Think of a story about one person in your family.

    ▶ Who is the story about? (What is his or her name?) _my mother_

    This story is about _the job my mother I like job in this town_

    ▶ Where does the story take place? (What is the name of the village, city or country?)

    This story takes place in _San luis la herradura is a town in the beach_

    ▶ When does the story happen? (Is it day or night? Is it summer, fall, winter or spring? What year does it happen?)

    The story happens in _Summer is day_.

3. Tell the story to your partner.

4. Listen as your partner tells you his or her story.

LESSON 1

ACTIVITY 4: Think About Today's Lesson

1. Reflect on what you learned. Finish the sentences.

   Today I learned _____

   _____

   _____

   _____.

   I plan to _____

   _____

   _____

   _____.

   A question I still have is _____

   _____

   _____

   _____.

2. Think about important words or ideas in this lesson. Read the words below. Draw a line to match the word and the definition.

   family story   a record of family members

   family tree or **family circle**   a family event

3. Review the ideas in the lesson.

   Lesson 1: Making Family Connections
   Telling family stories builds vocabulary and develops language skills. Family stories can be told in your home language or English or both. Family pictures help your family learn about its heritage. Creating a family picture helps your child learn to organize his or her thoughts.

LESSON 1

4. Are there other important points you learned from this lesson?
    - List them below.
    - Share your ideas with the class.

   _____

   _____

   _____

LESSON 1

 Take–Home Activity

Lesson 1: Making Family Connections

Goal
Tell family stories and share your family picture with your child.

Objectives

▶ Talk about your family circle or family tree with your child.

▶ Have fun sharing family stories with your child.

▶ Collect and bring things from home to help tell family stories to your classmates.

Directions

1. Prepare. Think about the following questions.

    ▶ Why did the teacher read you a story?

    ▶ What is a family story?

    ▶ What is a family circle?

    ▶ What is a family tree?

2. Try this at home.

    ▶ Share your family circle or family tree with your child.

    ▶ Tell a family story to your child.

    ▶ Ask your child to tell, write or draw a family story for you.

3. Review.

    ▶ Think about what you did with your child.

    ▶ Use your own words or the words in the boxes to help you answer the questions.

What did your child think of the family story you told?

My child thought the story was _____.

| Funny - Silly - Sad |

UNIT 3: Family Stories

LESSON 1

Does your child like to tell stories or hear stories?

My child _____.

> likes to tell stories.
> likes to hear stories.
> likes to tell and hear stories.

What did your child like best about the family circle or family tree?

My child liked _____

_____.

Write a sentence below to tell about the family story you shared with your child.

_____

_____.

Examples:
I told my child about her great–grandmother.
I told my family about her family in Nicaragua.
My child told me a story about fishing with her cousins.

Useful Words and Phrases

Verbs (past tense):	Nouns (people, places, things):	Prepositions:
• told • shared • explained	• story • family story • cousin • great–grandmother	• about • in • with

LESSON 1

4. Reflect.

   ▶ What did you and your child have fun doing?

   We had fun _____

   _____.

   ▶ What do you think your child learned?

   My child learned _____

   _____.

   ▶ How did your child respond when you told a family story?

   My child _____

   _____.

   ▶ What went well?

   _____

   _____ went well.

   ▶ What could go better next time?

   _____

   _____ could go better next time.

5. Prepare for the next class.

   ▶ Collect items that show some of your family events:
      - baby books
      - photo albums, pictures
      - family Bible
      - postcards from family or friends
      - birthday cards
      - recipe cards

   Family events include:
   - births
   - weddings
   - holiday celebrations
   - getting a family pet
   - reunions

   ▶ Bring the items to the next class.

UNIT 3: Family Stories 13

LESSON 1

 **Actividad para realizar en el hogar**

Lección 1: Comprender los vínculos familiares

Meta
Contar historias familiares y compartir fotos de familia con su niño.

Objetivos

- Conversar sobre su círculo o árbol familiar con su niño.
- Divertirse compartiendo historias familiares con su niño.
- Juntar y traer cosas de casa que le ayuden cuando les cuente las historias a sus compañeros.

Instrucciones

1. Prepárese. Piense en las siguientes preguntas.
   - ¿Por qué le leyó una historia el maestro?
   - ¿Qué es una historia familiar?
   - ¿Qué es un círculo familiar?
   - ¿Qué es un árbol familiar?

2. Para hacer en casa.
   - Comparta su árbol familiar con su niño.
   - Cuéntele una historia familiar al niño.
   - Pídale al niño que le cuente, escriba y dibuje una historia familiar.

3. Repase.
   - Piense en lo que hizo con su niño.
   - Utilice sus propias palabras que hay en las casillas para ayudarle con las preguntas.

   ¿Qué piensa su niño sobre la historia familiar que contó?

   Mi hijo pensó que la historia fue: _____

   | divertida - - - - - - - - - - - - - - - - - - - chistosa - triste |

14 Parenting for Academic Success

LESSON 1

¿Le gusta a su niño contar historias o escucharlas?

A mi niño _____.

> le gusta contar historias
> le gusta escuchar historias
> le gusta contar y escuchar historias

¿Qué es lo que más le gustó a su niño sobre el círculo o árbol familiar?

A mi niño le gustó _____

_____.

Escriba una oración para contar sobre la historia familiar que compartió con su niño.

_____

_____.

Ejemplos:
Le conté a mi niño sobre su bisabuela.
Le conté a mi niño sobre nuestra familia en Nicaragua.
Mi niño me contó una historia de cuando fue a pescar con sus primos.

Palabras y frases útiles		
Verbos (pasado): • dije • compartí • explique	Sustantivos (personas, lugares, cosas): • historia • historia familiar • primo • bisabuela	Preposiciones: • sobre • en • con

UNIT 3: Family Stories

LESSON 1

4. Reflexione.

   ▶ ¿Con qué actividad se divirtieron más usted y su niño?

   Nos divertimos _____
   _____.

   ▶ ¿Qué cree que aprendió su niño?

   Mi niño aprendió _____
   _____.

   ▶ ¿Como respondio su niño cuando le contó la historia familiar?

   Mi niño respondió _____
   _____.

   ▶ ¿Qué cosas resultaron bien?

   _____
   _____ resultaron bien.

   ▶ ¿Qué podría resultar mejor la próxima vez?

   _____
   _____ podría resultar mejor la próxima vez.

5. Prepárese para la próxima clase.

   ▶ Junte artículos que muestren algunos de sus acontecimientos familiares. Por ejemplo:
      • libros para bebés
      • álbumes de fotos, fotografías
      • Biblia familiar
      • postales de la familia o de amigos
      • tarjetas de cumpleaños
      • tarjetas con recetas de cocina

   ▶ Traiga estos artículos a su próxima clase.

Ejemplos de acontecimientos familiares:
• Nacimientos
• Matrimonios
• Celebración de los días de fiesta
• Llegada de un animal doméstico a la familia (perro, gato, etc.)
• Reuniones

Parenting for Academic Success

LESSON 2

 **LESSON 2: Sharing Family Stories**

Lesson Goal
Explore family stories as a way to help children learn about their culture, build their vocabulary and develop skills used in reading.

Lesson Objectives
Today we will:
- ▶ Listen to a family story about a home remedy.
- ▶ Compare family stories about a home remedy.
- ▶ Practice the simple past tense when telling family stories.
- ▶ Share family stories.
- ▶ Review and think about what we have learned together.

Lesson Warm-Up
1. What is your favorite family event?

   My favory historie is form my family chrismans is very happy all family for get the present in the reonion all family I like chrimmas.

2. Why is it important?

   chrimmas is impor for all familie reunion in one house is only day this reunion my famyly

Family Events
- births
- weddings
- holiday celebrations
- family reunions
- _____
- _____
- _____
- _____

UNIT 3: Family Stories

LESSON 2

 Points to Remember

Tell your child stories about family experiences and home remedies. It will help your child:

- Learn about his or her home culture.
- Learn to use words in new ways.
- Gain skills to read and write.

Can you add some more important points to this list?

_____

_____

_____

_____

LESSON 2

Activity 1: Key Vocabulary

Words in this lesson are listed below. Use the Key Vocabulary pages to build your vocabulary.

1. Review the words. Which ones do you know?

Word Part	Word	Example	Translation
noun	earache		dolor Oido
noun	home remedies		Ramedio casero Ruda
noun	family heritage		El salvador Irencia familiar
noun	oral tradition		Historia tradicion
noun	childhood memory		Historia de Pequeño
verb	ignited		ensender la llama de
verb	rolled		silindiar Rodando masa
verb	placed		Espacio colocar
verb	threw		tirar
verb	took		hablar tomar
verb	went		fue in

UNIT 3: Family Stories

LESSON 2

2. Practice Key Vocabulary words. Listen to the word in a sentence.
   ▶ Guess the meaning of the word.
   ▶ Write a new sentence with the word.

Example: *Placed: Mother placed the food on the table.*

Key Vocabulary Words:

I have an earoche _____

_____ _____

_____ _____

_____ _____

Key Vocabulary Sentences:

I have an earache

yestarday I made cup home remedies.

My grammother Last yers familie heritage

I took went my mom her poiment in you old hospital

Yestarday my sister reade old story remember chilhood m

My doughter ignited the stove in house

In My house small (placed) for

Last week took icrem.

Parenting for Academic Success

Activity 2: A Family Story about a Home Remedy

1. Listen as your teacher reads this story.

Earache Treatment

I remember watching my mother and father go out to the front porch with a bucket of water. My mother took a sheet of newspaper, rolled it up into a cone shape and placed it on my father's ear. She kept telling us to stay back. She very briefly ignited the paper, then threw it into the water to extinguish it. I was amazed.

You see, my father would sometimes get water trapped in his outer ear when he went swimming, because of an injury when he was in the Navy during World War II. This treatment, called *ventosa*, would create a vacuum and evaporate the water.

> Reprinted with permission of the publisher, Children's Book Press, San Francisco, CA, www.childrensbookpress.org. *In My Family/En mi familia* copyright © 1996 by Carmen Lomas Garza.

2. What home remedy did the mother use?

    ▶ The mother used a home remedy called ___Ventosa___.

3. What problem did the mother's home remedy treat?

    ▶ The home remedy treated ___Ventosa vacuum evaporate___.

4. What home remedy do you remember?

Problem	Home Remedy
Example: A bee stung me.	**Example:** My mother put mud on my bee sting.

UNIT 3: Family Stories

LESSON 2

5. What home remedy do you use now?

Problem	Home Remedy
Example: My son's stomach <u>is</u> upset.	**Example:** I <u>give</u> him some vinegar in water.
Pecto Bismoll	NO

6. Read the story. Fill in the missing words.
   ▸ Use the words in the box.
   ▸ Look back at the *Earache Treatment* story if you need help.

Simple Past Tense	
Regular (verb + *ed* ending)	*Irregular*
• rolled	• took *tomar*
• placed	• threw *tirar*
• ignited	• was/were
• trapped	• went

Earache Treatment

I remember watching my mother and father go out to the front porch with a bucket of water. My mother __took__ a sheet of newspaper, __rolled__ it up into a cone shape and __threw__ (placed) it on my father's ear. She kept telling us to stay back. She very briefly __ignited__ the paper, then __trapped__ (threw) it into the water to extinguish it. I __was__ amazed.

You see, my father would sometimes get water __trapped__ in his outer ear when he __went__ swimming, because of an injury when he __was__ in the Navy during World War II. This treatment, called *ventosa*, would create a vacuum and evaporate the water.

Reprinted with permission of the publisher, Children's Book Press, San Francisco, CA, www.childrensbookpress.org. *In My Family/En mi familia* copyright © 1996 by Carmen Lomas Garza.

LESSON 2

7. Write a sentence about a home remedy in your family. Use the simple past tense.
    ▶ Share your sentence with a partner. Then share it with the class.
    ▶ Listen to your classmates share their home remedies.
    ▶ Compare home remedies.

> **Example**:
> My mother put mud on my bee sting.
> The mud took away the pain.

_____

_____

_____

LESSON 2

Activity 3: Sharing Family Stories

1. Is there a family story you like to tell? What is it?

    ▶ I remember when _____

    _____.

    ▶ If you need help, tell a story about:
    - a home remedy
    - a family event
    - your child
    - a family tradition

2. Draw pictures to help you remember the story.

3. Give your story a title.

   _____

   _____

4. Tell your story to the group. Use English or your home language or both.
    ▶ Remember to use the past tense to tell a story that happened in the past.

   > **Example**:
   > When I <u>was</u> five, we <u>left</u> El Salvador and <u>moved</u> to New York.
   > My child <u>lived</u> with my mother when I <u>worked</u> in California.
   > When my child <u>was</u> little, she <u>played</u> with her cousins in Puerto Rico.

5. Listen as your classmates tell their stories.

UNIT 3: Family Stories

LESSON 2

Activity 4: Tell a Family Story to Your Classmates

1. Think about the family stories that your group shared.
    - Which story did you like?
    - What did you like about the story?

2. Pick one story from your group to share with the class.
    - Each person in your group should prepare to share the story.
    - Listen as other groups share their stories.

ACTIVITY 5: Think About Today's Lesson

1. Reflect on what you learned. Finish the sentences.

   Today I learned _____

   _____

   _____

   _____ .

   I plan to _____

   _____

   _____

   _____ .

   A question I still have is _____

   _____

   _____

   _____ .

2. Think about important words or ideas in this lesson.
   ▸ Read the words.
   ▸ Talk about what they mean.
   ▸ Add words you want to remember.

   - home remedy
   - oral tradition
   - family tradition
   - childhood memory
   -
   -

UNIT 3: Family Stories

LESSON 2

3. Review the ideas in the lesson.

   Lesson 2: Sharing Family Stories
   When you and your child share family stories, your child learns many things about your culture. He or she also learns many things that will help him or her in school.

   When families tell family stories together, children:
   - Learn about their family heritage.
   - Take pride in their family and culture.
   - Understand the way stories begin, develop and end.
   - Speak and listen in their home language at a high level.
   - Learn to organize their thinking.

4. Do you have any other important ideas you learned from this lesson?
   ▸ List them below.
   ▸ Share your ideas with the class.

   _____

   _____

   _____

   _____

LESSON 2

 Take-Home Activity

Lesson 2: Sharing Family Stories

Goal
Help your child develop language skills by sharing family stories and family experiences.

Objectives

- Tell family stories with your child.
- Tell your child about a home remedy your family used when you were a child.
- Remind your child about a home remedy you use now.
- Help your child tell a family story.

Directions

1. Prepare. Think about the following questions.
   - What story did you tell in class?
     - Listen to your tape-recorded story.
     - Recall the story you told in class. Look at the picture you drew.
   - When do you plan to tell that story to your child?
   - How will you explain home remedies to your child?
   - How will you tell your child when to use home remedies?

2. Try this at home.
   - Share your family story with your child.
     - If you tape-recorded your story, play the tape for your child.
     - If you drew pictures, share your pictures with your child.
   - Tell more family stories with your child.
   - Optional: record a family story with your child.
   - Optional: draw pictures of your family story with your child.
   - Optional: begin a family journal with your child. Record family stories in the journal. Include pictures your child draws or photographs of things you did together. Include stories from you and stories from your child.

3. Review.
   - Think about what you did with your child.
     - Did your child share a story with you?
     - How does sharing stories with your child help his or her reading skills?
     - Was it hard to find a time to share a story with your child?

UNIT 3: Family Stories

LESSON 2

▶ Write a sentence to tell what you did this week. Use the examples to help you.

_____

_____.

> **Examples**:
> We listened to a tape–recorded family story.
> We talked about the pictures of a family story.
> I told our children about our family in Costa Rica.
> My child told me a story about his friend at school.

Useful Words and Phrases		
Verbs (past tense): • listened • talked • told • shared • looked	Nouns (people, places, things): • story • family story • friend • cousin • great–grandmother	Prepositions: • about • to • in • at

4. Reflect.

   ▶ What did you and your child have fun doing?

   We had fun _____

   _____.

   ▶ What do you think your child learned?

   My child learned _____

   _____.

   ▶ What went well?

   _____

   _____ went well.

   ▶ What could go better next time?

   _____

   _____ could go better next time.

30   Parenting for Academic Success

LESSON 2

Actividad para realizar en el hogar

LECCIÓN 2: Compartir historias familiares

Meta
Ayudar a los niños a desarrollar sus habilidades lingüísticas, compartiendo historias y experiencias familiares.

Objetivos
- Contar historias familiares con su niño.
- Contarle al niño sobre un remedio casero que su familia usaba en su niñez.
- Recordarle al niño sobre algún remedio casero que usted usa actualmente.
- Ayudarle a contar una historia familiar.

Instrucciones
1. Prepárese. Piense en las siguientes preguntas.
    - ¿Qué historia contó en la clase?
        - Escuche la historia grabada.
        - Recuerde la historia que usted contó en clase, mirando los dibujos que hizo.
    - ¿Cuándo planea contarle esa historia a su niño?
    - ¿Cómo le va a explicar lo que son los remedios caseros?
    - ¿Cómo le va a explicar a su niño en qué situación se debieran usar los remedios caseros?

2. Para hacer en casa.
    - Comparta su historia familiar con su niño.
        - Si grabo su historia, ponga el casete para que lo escuche el niño.
        - Si dibujó ilustraciones para contar su historia, muéstrele los dibujos a su niño.
    - Cuenten más historias familiares con su niño.
    - Opcional: grabe una historia familiar con su niño.
    - Opcional: haga dibujos con su niño sobre su historia familiar.
    - Opcional: comience un diario de vida familiar con su niño. Documente historias familiares en el diario. Incluya ilustraciones que dibuje su niño o fotografías de cosas que hayan hecho juntos. Incluya historias suyas y de su niño.

3. Repase.
    - Piense acerca de lo que hizo con su niño.
        - ¿Compartió su niño una historia con usted?
        - ¿Cómo le ayuda al niño en sus habilidades de lectura en contar y compartir historias?
        - ¿Fue difícil encontrar tiempo para contarle una historia al niño?

UNIT 3: Family Stories

LESSON 2

▶ Escribe una oración acerca de lo que hizo durante la semana. Los ejemplos le pueden ayudar.

_____

_____.

> **Ejemplos:**
> Escuchamos la historia familiar grabada en casete.
> Conversamos sobre las fotografías de la historia familiar.
> Le conté a mis hijos sobre nuestra familia en Costa Rica.
> Mi niño me contó una historia sobre su amigo de la escuela.

Palabras y frases útiles		
Verbos (pasado): • escuchó • habló • dije • compartí • miré	Sustantivos (personas, lugares, cosas): • historia • historia familiar • amigo • primo • bisabuela	Preposiciones: • sobre • a • en

4. Reflexione.

   ▶ ¿Con qué actividad se divirtieron más usted y su niño?

   Nos divertimos _____

   _____.

   ▶ ¿Qué cree que aprendió su niño?

   Mi niño aprendió _____

   _____.

   ▶ ¿Qué cosas resultaron bien?

   _____

   _____ resultaron bien.

   ▶ ¿Qué podría resultar mejor la próxima vez?

   _____

   _____ podría resultar mejor la próxima vez.

Parent Survey

This survey is to evaluate the unit on **Family Stories**. There are no wrong answers and you will not be asked to talk about your answers.

1. What information did you learn from the Family Stories unit?

   _____

   _____

   _____

2. What else would you like to know about the Family Stories unit?

   _____

   _____

   _____

3. How will the information help you help your child?

   _____

   _____

   _____

4. Check (✔) one of the following statements about this unit.

   _____ I understood everything.

   _____ I understood most of it.

   _____ I understood some of it.

   _____ I understood a little of it.

   _____ I did not understand any of it.

When you have finished this survey, please give it to your teacher.

ENCUESTA A LOS PADRES

Esta encuesta es para evaluar la unidad de las **Historias familiares**. No existen respuestas incorrectas y no se le pedirá que comente lo que respondió.

1. ¿Qué cosas aprendió en la unidad de las Historias familiares?

   _____

   _____

   _____

2. ¿Qué otras cosas le gustarían saber acerca de la unidad de las Historias familiares?

   _____

   _____

   _____

3. ¿De qué manera le ayudará a usted esta información para poder ayudar a su niño?

   _____

   _____

   _____

4. Marque (✔) sólo una de las siguientes afirmaciones sobre esta unidad.

   _____ Entendí todo.

   _____ Entendí la mayoría de las cosas.

   _____ Entendí algunas cosas.

   _____ Entendí un poco.

   _____ No entendí en absoluto.

   Cuando haya finalizado esta encuesta, entréguesela a su maestro.